I Quit!
Oh wait, I'm the Mom
A practical guide to finding your joy again

Michelle McVittie

◆ FriesenPress

Suite 300 - 990 Fort St
Victoria, BC, V8V 3K2
Canada

www.friesenpress.com

Copyright © 2018 by Michelle McVittie
First Edition — 2018

All rights reserved.

No part of this publication may be reproduced in any form, or by any means, electronic or mechanical, including photocopying, recording, or any information browsing, storage, or retrieval system, without permission in writing from FriesenPress.

ISBN
978-1-5255-2703-6 (Hardcover)
978-1-5255-2704-3 (Paperback)
978-1-5255-2705-0 (eBook)

1. Family & Relationships, Parenting

Distributed to the trade by The Ingram Book Company

Table of Contents

Don't Lose Yourself in Motherhood 1

My New Motto 15

How do I Find Time for Myself, When Everyone Around Me Needs Me? 19

Loving Yourself 29

Mother's Guilt: The Silent Killer 35

No One has Time You Have to Make Time 43

Start from the Outside and Work Your Way In 49

Get Moving! 57

Clear Your Head of All the Clutter 63

Don't Be So Hard on Yourself 73

Find Like-Minded People 77

Think Positive 81

There are People Out There Who Can Help You They Make a Living Out of It 91

Ask for What You Need 97

You Don't Have to Do It All 105

Delegate! 111

Anything is Possible You Just Have to Try 117

I'm not really going to quit,
I just wonder what would happen if I did?

Michelle McVittie

Stressed?

I'm not stressed.

I just need a small break.

When the Stress of Motherhood Finally Adds Up

Don't Lose Yourself in Motherhood

Motherhood can be such a blessing, when we aren't too tired to appreciate it. Do you feel as though you're barely keeping your head above water? Do you wonder what would happen if you decided to go on an unplanned vacation, all by yourself? Parenting *can* be done without losing yourself; the first step is realizing **YOU DON'T HAVE TO DO IT ALL**. The second step is **making yourself a priority**. Seems impossible?

Life didn't change because other people changed, it changed because I changed.

I felt the same. I wanted things to be different, but I didn't know how. I noticed how quickly I would say no to myself instead of saying no to work, the dishes or family commitments. Instead of allowing my resentment to grow, I changed my priorities. **It started with me**. I started doing things that made me feel happy, that filled my cup, and life became calmer and happier. Life didn't change because other people changed, it changed because I changed. I looked at the world differently; my perspective was more positive. I took my foot off the gas and slowed down and appreciated the little things in life. I enjoyed my coffee in peace. I watched a small child playing in wonderment. I admired nature and listened to the laughter of my children. **I found my joy**. My obligations for others shifted to my self-care, and then I had more energy for those most important to me. I changed how I reacted to stressors, life and the people around me. I took my control back. You have no control over other people; you only have control over how you react. When you start reacting differently, people change how they react to you, for the better. It's possible, I know because I've done it.

You have no control over other people; you only have control over how you react.

I'm learning to enjoy the process of making myself a priority

Be present in the moment. We tend to look ahead and miss the here and now. The end result is the focus, but the "in between" is the best part. Your target may change; go with it. Perhaps the final destination isn't meant for you. The journey may bring you down a different path. But if your heart is set on a fixed result, you miss the experience and learning on the way there.

> You can't pour from an empty cup
>
> It's time for a refill

Find peace within and everything else will follow

In an airplane you put the oxygen mask on yourself first, then your child. In life we tend to do the opposite. Self-care should be your first priority; most moms don't even consider this an option. I hear many complaints that there isn't enough time in the day. You're right, there is NEVER enough time. You have to make time. You can do this; just take it one step at a time.

You can do this; just take it one step at a time.

I know firsthand how hard it is, because I'm a recovering "Supermom Wannabe". I needed to be everything to everyone, except myself. In the end nothing really measured up. I was tired, and my house was a mess. I felt overwhelmed and unorganized. I knew there was more to life than this. I needed to stop setting myself up for failure, so I started to be real. **I remembered I was a person before I was a mom**. I redefined myself as Michelle the writer, the friend, the crafting queen, the athlete, mother, sister, daughter and wife. Life started feeling more fulfilling. I made myself a priority and I felt alive, happy and comfortable again. When things came up in my life that were stressful or unplanned I was better able to cope, because my stress level was lower. If you're constantly sitting at a four out of ten on the stress meter, it doesn't take long for your head to pop off.

You're right, there is
NEVER enough time,
you have to make time.

> Don't lose yourself in motherhood. You deserve to be your own person.

How do you define yourself? How can you rewrite the definition?

Take a moment to think of a few words to define who you are. If you are struggling, think about who you were before children, or what you aspire to be. What are your interests? Personality traits you admire? Our brain is automatically programmed to think of the negative first. If you're finding this difficult, ask your children, your partner, or a close friend. They will be able to give you the positive perspective you're looking for.

Here are a few suggestions:

> Funny, fun, spontaneous, thoughtful, inspiring, kind, caring, creative, loving, feisty, witty, adventurous, smart, strong, resilient, tenacious, energetic, brave, bold, daring, exciting, calm, compassionate, resourceful, artistic, charismatic, compelling, alluring, magnetic, charming, captivating, entertaining, clever, innovative, driven, compelling, motivated, focused, energetic, sincere, genuine, generous, spontaneous, successful, powerful, amazing, passionate, empowering, independent, enthusiastic, influential, determined

My New Motto

My Life Mantra

Shut Up

None of your business

Walk Away!

Repeat after me: I don't have to do it all, I don't have to fix it, walk away!

The people around you can figure things out on their own, including your children (we will get to them later). I am a chronic good listener and advice giver. It's not always a bad thing, but I gave it too much of my time, and it drained me of my energy. I felt I was going out of my way to be kind, but people didn't always take it that way. I got offended when they didn't care what I had to say, or wouldn't follow my advice. So I stopped... yup, cold turkey. I stopped, and it felt liberating. I assumed people wanted my advice, even the ones who didn't ask for it. To tell you the truth when I'm venting, I want to do just that. I want to be heard to be validated. I'm really not looking for advice. However, I felt that I should give advice to those around me, even someone I just met.

I remember the first time I decided to walk away. I was at the salon, a calm and relaxing place for me. The only problem is you can't control who else is there. For most people, hairdressers are like therapists, so everyone tells them their stories, and I would get caught in the crossfire. I was waiting to be seen, and one girl was talking about her boyfriend and how he was treating her (not a nice guy, clearly not into her, not worth her time and effort). I thought this all in my head. Another patron sitting close by took my old role for me. She offered advice because she had been with her boyfriend for seven years on and off, and she knew what would be best. I thought, *Oh honey, really you think you have this?* I caught my judgement and feelings of irritation. I took a deep breath, told myself, *Shut up, it's none of your business. Just walk away!* It felt fantastic.

Repeat after me: I don't have to do it all, I don't have to fix it, walk away!

The more often I walk away the calmer I am. Did I really need the weight of the world on my shoulders? I don't miss it. When I do offer a shoulder to cry on or some friendly advice, I do it because I want to, not because I feel I need to. I only have so much energy to give, I choose whom I give to with sincere consideration. This new practice has helped me live a calmer life.

How do I Find Time for Myself, When Everyone Around Me Needs Me?

Before children I had it ALL figured out. They DID NOT follow the plan!

When I became a mother my role was the selfless caregiver

Growing up, I came home from a day outside with my friends when the street lights came on, and I'm still alive to talk about it. Having this freedom away from my parent's watchful eye gave me many skills. I learned about time management, problem solving, conflict resolution, street smarts, and most of all INDEPENDENCE! There is an epidemic of **hyper parenting** that is running mothers into the ground. Our society expects parents to supervise and engage their children around the clock. To save time and possible shaming from the world, parents – especially moms – end up doing everything for their children, no matter their age or abilities. The fear of allowing children to do things for themselves and try new things, leads to children and teens who lack life skills, independence and confidence. Some may even say it's what causes the sense of entitlement in our youth today. In the end our children learn to depend on us, they get the message that they do not have the skills to take care of things themselves. As they grow up they will have less confidence to try new things, and to be independent.

There is an epidemic of hyper parenting that is running mothers into the ground.

There has to be a healthy balance. You have to be able to step back, to fight the urge to protect your child all the time. As your children grow, you have to start preparing them for life. Ask yourself, **am I protecting or am I preparing them?** You protect infants and toddlers. You have to be able to tolerate the distress in yourself. You have to be able to tolerate the distress in your children. That comes from self-care. From being calm yourself. Children learn what they live. If they know you will always rescue them and fix things, they will always expect you to fulfill that role. I'm not saying to drop them into the deep end and expect them to figure it out. You show them how to do things and then slowly step back. Fight the urge to take over, to fix. You will be giving the gift of independence. You will give the message: I know you can do this!

The fact that you are reading this book right now, shows you want a change. It shows you want more out of life.

Children learn what they live. If they know you always rescue them and fix things, they will always expect you to fulfill that role.

The time is now

First things first, **there is no such thing as a SUPERMOM!** It's just like the monster under the bed – we've never seen it, but we all believed it was there. When I was five, I jumped from the door to my bed every night; it was a waste of time. There was no troll under my bed that magically appeared in the dark. But I believed it was there, so I continued to jump. I have been doing a lot of unnecessary jumping in different stages of my life. I set high standards for myself with friends, boyfriends, in my career, as a wife, and now as a mother. Staying motivated and striving to do better is not a poor quality. The problem is when you are doing it for the wrong reasons.

Are you setting unrealistic goals?

Do you push yourself beyond your limits for the sake of others?

Are you always saying yes to others, but actually saying no to yourself?

When I became a mother I tried to be something that was impossible, I tried to be perfect. I tried really hard, but never felt like I measured up. I didn't measure up because my house was never clean enough, I wasn't organized, even my cupcake icing skills sucked... among many other things I judged myself harshly for.

Why do we feel like society's ever-changing expectations need to be our expectations? I could either listen to all the different opinions out there, **or listen to my heart.** I chose to say "**I'm good enough** and what other people think is *their* business, not mine." I don't need to take on society's values as my own. I need to focus on my own personal goals and values. Looking back, I know **I was the best I could be**. I struggled because I didn't have the tools I needed. Tools I slowly started developing, tools that have empowered and grounded me. These tools have helped me make myself a priority. I learned to get myself and my family organized and focused on the things that really mattered. I was there; I'm still finding me. I hope I never stop working at it. Each phase of your life should push you to renegotiate your expectations.

"I'm good enough and what other people think is their business, not mine."

Today I choose positivity.

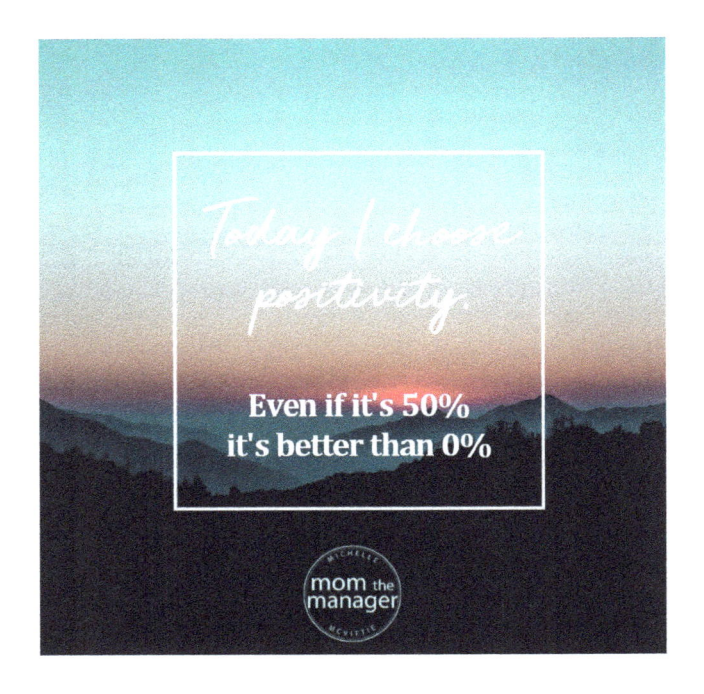

Even if it's 50% it's better than 0%

Loving Yourself

It's hard to feel good enough. Social media just adds fuel to the fire. It provides an easy venue to have other people's success shoved in your face. I can easily turn on my phone and see how well everyone **appears** to be functioning. When looking at a perfect selfie I never thought, *Maybe it was taken twenty times before it was posted?* There were many people I viewed as "perfect", but did they actually exist?

It was hard not to envy those "Supermoms" who looked like they had it all. It was hard not to compare myself to what other women appeared to have. I have been comparing myself since Grade 7, how do I stop that cycle now?

The mothers of social media looked great. They clearly made time for workouts, play dates and nights out with friends. Their homes were impeccable, and their children were dressed in matching stylish outfits and were well behaved. I made all these assumptions from what I saw in pictures. I made these observations while at the park, coffee shops and other social events. I felt like I was missing something. How did they pull it off? Then one day someone commented on how they admired me. I was shocked. In someone else's eyes, I may have it all; I might be doing something that other women wish they could do. What I disliked about myself, they didn't notice. It was my own self-criticism. I had to make a change. It was killing my spirit; I was constantly complaining. Who wants to be around someone like that? I didn't, but I was becoming one of those people. I lost sight of what was important. I focused on what I didn't have instead of what I was blessed with. I quit complaining cold turkey. I needed to do it for me. I realized **my best is good enough. I'm not perfect; I'm human.**

When looking at a perfect selfie I never thought; maybe it was taken twenty times before it was posted? There were many people I viewed as "perfect", but did they actually exist?

I made this change for myself and for my children. **Children learn what they live**. I wanted to be a good example. I didn't want my kids, especially my daughter to hear me talking poorly about myself. This message comes from us. It made me re-evaluate what was really important.

> I do the best I can. Some days I try a little harder, other days not so much.

Start focusing on what you do have, instead of what you don't have. "The grass is always greener on the other side of the fence" is an age old saying, because this has been a reality for society since the beginning of time.

This simple exercise can help you start focusing on what really matters.

I am happy for _____
I am happy for _____
I am happy for _____

I am grateful for _____
I am grateful for _____
I am grateful for _____

Try to do this on a regular basis. You may want to have a notebook to write it down. It could be something you do every day, every second day or on a weekly basis. It's easier to do at first. The struggle is coming up with new things to be grateful for the longer you do the exercise.

Mother's Guilt: The Silent Killer

Mother's Guilt:

It's a silent killer.
You need to let it go!
It's only holding you back.

I love being a mom. I just didn't realize the emotional baggage that came along with it. It's called **mother's guilt**. It's a silent killer. It replaces logical thinking, with a voice that tells you:

- "Do better!"
- "They are only young once."
- "They need me."
- "I can't let them do that on their own."
- "I hate to see them cry."
- "It's better when Mommy does it."
- "I can't take a break."
- "I can't leave them."

The list could go on and on. Can you relate to any of them, or all of them? The key is to catch the thoughts and tell them to shut up. Be prepared for the thoughts and have a comeback. Here are a few suggestions:

- "You don't have to do it all."
- "They will survive if Daddy puts them to bed tonight."
- "If I go to yoga class I will feel better and have more energy to love them when I get back."

> "Only mommy can do it."
>
> "It has to be mom."
>
> "Mom does it best."
>
> NOPE!
> It's a trap. Walk away.
> You DO NOT
> need to
> do it ALL.

This silent killer stops you from taking care of yourself and your needs. **Before you became a parent you were a person, but that person gets buried for years until the children are grown. At that point you forget how to be you.**

Before you became a mom, you were a person. Remember Her?

I decided to take a stand. I wanted my children to be my joy; I didn't want to resent them. I wanted to be a mom who had it all and didn't feel as though I gave up my identity, or my sense of self with motherhood. I quickly realized that my children didn't take away my sense of self – I allowed it to happen. **I had the power to make it stop and take the control back. I could choose to do it all, to forgo self-care, to lose myself OR make a change. It was time to make a change, but it wouldn't be easy.**

Before you became a parent you were a person, but that person gets buried for years until the children are grown. At that point you forget how to be you.

Now it's your turn to **take your life back**. Being a mother is a great gift, but you can't enjoy it when you feel as though you're barely keeping your head above water.

No One has Time You Have to Make Time

My floors may be sticky, but I always find time for myself!

If I got a dollar every time I heard "I don't have time", I would be living on my own private island right now. No one has time. You have to make it a priority. **My floors may be sticky, but I always make time for myself.**

I know it's hard, I'm also a mom. If I can do it, so can you. Moms can be their own worst enemy. Why do you have to do it all? Do the kids really need to be put to bed in a certain way? Do you have to stay in all the time?

You don't have to make the cupcakes from scratch, or clean the house on your own! You don't have to wash the laundry, fold it AND put it all away by yourself.

If you do everything for everyone else, you are letting them know that this is what they can expect from you. Work together as a family: **Team Family!** When you work together, there is more time for **Family Time.** Life passes by quickly. I'd rather be hanging out with my children, than staying home so I can catch up on whatever I feel needs to get done. The message we unintentionally send is that stuff/chores/duties are more important. I'm not suggesting you just quit responsibility and go play at the park. I'm just suggesting there can be another way. **Start with putting your guilt away and make a plan to do things differently.**

Work together as a family: Team Family! When you work together, there is more time for Family Time.

Getting organized

There Will Never be Enough Time.

Make the Time.

Prioritize Self-Care

No one has enough time in their day; you have to get organized to be more productive. Make goals, make a plan, and write it down! I struggle with time management and organization. I had to learn how to stop wasting so much time, I felt like a hamster on a wheel. I started reading articles and books on how to get organized and keep a clean home. The advice was simple: when you walk in the door put your keys, shoes, coat and purse away, right away. Put everything back in the same spot each time. Everything needs a place. That's it? No magical secrets that were kept from me my whole life? Just put it away, right away? I tried it... It worked! The more organized I became, the less time I wasted and the more time I actually had for myself.

I got an old fashioned agenda. You know, the paper kind. My phone doesn't show me everything all at once. My new agenda is my lifeline. I make lists for what I need to do, what appointments I have, and which child I'm dropping off at what activity each day. From my master list, I make a list of three to four things I want to accomplish each day.

I started a morning and bedtime routine. It may seem silly, but I needed one. The purpose of a routine is to make priorities of what needs to get done. Once you have a routine set and you practice it on a regular basis, it becomes second nature. Less time is wasted, you get your work done and you feel more in control and organized.

Here is a sample of what mine looks like:

Morning:
- positive affirmation
- don't touch your phone
- make coffee
- load the dishwasher
- drink water
- take iron pill
- check to do list
- pick top three to accomplish today

Evening:
- load the dishwasher
- wipe down the kitchen sink and counter
- make my lunch
- check what I have to do for the next day
- 10 minute tidy before bed
- get to bed at a decent hour

Now it's your turn to think about what your goals are. What is a priority? You may already have a clean home, but you haven't spent any time with your friends or partner in months. What routines do you have set? What new routines can you improve on or build on? When you make a plan and put things into your agenda or daily routine, they are more likely to get done.

Start from the Outside and Work Your Way In

How to Live a Healthier Lifestyle

1. Sleep more

2. Be active

3. Eat Healthy

4. Drink less caffeine

(Disregard #4, that can't be right!)

Go to the doctor; get a yearly physical. Make sure everything is in working order. Last year, after a routine physical my doctor ordered blood work. That physical changed my life. They discovered my iron was low. Within weeks, I felt so much better, I felt awake, and I felt alive. I used to think coffee was what I needed to survive, nope, it was iron pills. It was a relief to find out I could easily feel better. I was starting to think my constant state of fatigue was normal (at this point my children had been sleeping through the night for years, so I should not have felt so tired).

The doctor needs to know about your physical and mental health concerns. They are there to help you, but if you don't share your concerns they will never know you need help.

Get sleep. Set a timer, make a bedtime routine. Don't clean the floors an hour before bed, it will wind you up. TV and screen time are stimulants, shut them off at least an hour before bed. What do you do that relaxes you? If you don't know, make a list.

Use the list below to help you. Check off anything you like to do or would like to try. Add your own suggestions.

- Take a bath
- Play with a pet
- Read
- Draw or colour in a picture
- Crossword
- Word search
- Knitting or crochet
- Meditation
- Progressive muscle relaxation
- Take a nap
- Mental imagery
- Squeeze a stress ball
- Play with some rice
- Drink some herbal tea
- Listen to relaxing music
- Brush your hair
- Get into nature
- Creative visualization
- Create a quiet or Zen zone
- Stretch
- Write
- Yoga
- Smell something relaxing such as lavender or vanilla
- Texture: feather, smooth rock, a warm fuzzy blanket
- Drink some herbal tea
- Start a positivity journal (A place to remind you of all the good things. Positive words, inspiring quotes, love letters to yourself, goals, or things you are grateful for.)

The doctor needs to know about your physical and mental health concerns. They are there to help you, but if you don't share your concerns they will never know you need help.

Once you decide what you'd like to do, make it part of your routine, or pick a few days a week that you will make it happen. Work it out with your family, and with your partner so everyone knows the plan. It's not fun to get into a tub only to have the children banging on the door five minutes later, or climbing in with you! Announce what you are doing. Explain that *when* you get some quiet *then* you will spend some time with them. Remind them of the plan before you go. Set a timer if you need to. Put a sign on the door. Visuals are great reminders. Just make it happen.

STOP! Mommy Break Ahead
STOP! Mommy Break Ahead
STOP! Mommy Break Ahead
STOP! Mommy Break Ahead
STOP! Mommy Break Ahead
STOP! Mommy Break Ahead
STOP! Mommy Break Ahead
STOP! Mommy Break Ahead

To set the tone, I have written a special story just for you. Take a moment to enjoy the peace and relaxation in your imagination.

Mental Imagery Script: A Mother's Vacation

Today is a day like no other. Today you woke up well rested and refreshed. You take your time to enjoy the pleasure of waking up slowly and in complete silence. Your hotel room is luxurious and serene. The crisp white linens smell fresh and are soft against your skin. When you open your eyes a quiet calm comes over you. Take a deep breath and inhale relaxation. Breathe out any stress or guilt you may have. Breathe in peace, breath out chaos and stress.

You have a panoramic view of the ocean; you can hear the waves splashing down on the beach outside of your balcony. Each time a wave washes over the sand, you take another calming breath, enjoying the rhythmic song of the waves below. The warm sun streams through the patio doors and warms your face. You can feel the breeze wafting through the open patio doors. The calming environment fills your body with comfort and relaxation.

As you stand up, you take time to stretch before you walk out to the balcony. Your feet feel the warmth of the patio beneath you. You stop to look at the vast ocean and mountains in the distance. Take a deep breath in through your nose and out through your mouth. Say to yourself, "I deserve this time, I'm worth it." If any thoughts come into your head acknowledge them, but don't focus on them. Let them drift out of your mind and focus back on your breathing. Take a moment to drink in the sights, to feel the warm breeze kiss your shoulders and smell the ocean water. Repeat to yourself, "I am calm, I am relaxed, and I deserve this break." Take as long as you need to stay in this beautiful oasis. Remember, you can come back to this place whenever you need to.

Get Moving!

> "I work out so I can be a better me and a calmer mom. And so I can have dessert with NO REGRETS!"
>
> Michelle McVittie

I've always been an active person. But my idea of working out was walking to the corner store instead of driving. When my second child was six weeks old, a friend recommended a great trainer, and I started stroller fit class. Somehow, I motivated myself to get to class. The trainer started the class with a reminder to the post-partum moms that they needed to have permission from their doctor before they could start working out. I thought, is this a sign to run away? I am barely recovering from my C-section, I have a three-year-old in tow and here I am ready to put my body through more torture.

Everything jiggled when I moved, nothing felt good. I remember thinking, *Can I get a full body Spanx leotard?* The funny thing was, I went back the following week. I liked the social part of working out and I could relate to all the other moms around me.

Each week I went back, I loved it more and more. The socialization was nice; I missed talking to other grown-ups. These women were great, we laughed together, sweat together and would meet up for coffee throughout the week.

I quickly learned that exercise gave me the push I needed to take care of myself. I felt empowered by my new strength, my new body, and my new support system.

Find what will work for you. It might be taking a walk after dinner every night, finding a good app or YouTuber. Joining something with a friend always helps. If you have a workout buddy it makes it less intimidating to try a new thing. You push each other to follow through. You also have your own personal cheering squad! Whatever you choose, make a plan and follow through.

The more you take care of yourself the less stress you'll have, the better you'll sleep and your mood will improve. Find something you like. You may have to try a whole bunch of things until you find the one you like best. I've done: soccer, indoor and outdoor (co-ed and women only), yoga, stroller fit, boot camp, boxing, tennis, golf, running, hiking, swimming, aerobics, the gym, various classes at the gym, water aerobics, and running the stairs.

I like to try new things. If I'm not having fun, I move on to the next activity. What I've learned is that I like to be challenged. I am a social exerciser, and I like to have fun while working out. I always plan ahead and put the workout in my head the night before. So even if it's raining or I don't feel like it, I still go.

How do you get motivated? Maybe it's training for your first 5km race, or joining a social media group or a weight loss challenge. My cousin asked me to be part of her team for a charity. Instead of running a race, you climbed stairs at a football stadium. So I started doing the local stairs to train, and I ended up loving it. It was torture, but each time I went back it got better. I felt empowered. I felt as though I had won against something that told me I couldn't do it. And really, when you go to the bottom of the stairs you have no choice but to go back up. With people behind you there is no quitting. I was really shocked that I continued going back after the charity event was over.

Whatever you choose, make a plan and follow through.

The summer I went back to playing tennis was so much fun. I met great people, pushed myself outside my comfort zone and made a commitment to go every Sunday for novice co-ed doubles.

Working out for me needs to be social, I don't like working out alone. I love it when people know my name when I walk through the door at the gym. I do best with a workout partner. What works for you? Just try something. If it's too expensive, see if you can find it for free or maybe a cheaper version at a community centre for example. Wag jag, Groupon, etc. or "try it for free deal". If you can't find a sitter, find something like stroller fit to bring the kids along or trade babysitting services with a friend. Just get out and do something. Put a reminder in your phone, announce it on social media, or put a Post-it note on your bathroom mirror. Once you find the thing you like it won't feel like work anymore, I promise.

If you don't prioritize, things will not change.

Clear Your Head of All the Clutter

Mommy Brain Moments

The remote control went missing.
I checked in the usual spots:

bathroom

kitchen

pantry

There are days I think I'm losing my mind. I find the remote in the kitchen, I spend ten minutes looking for my keys and they are in my hand. I double check the door that I locked twenty seconds ago because I can't remember if I did it. I wash my hair three times, because I can't be sure if it was the second rinse or the first. On the days I have nothing planned and the phone rings I wonder, is it someone calling to see why I haven't shown up? I can go on and on. At one point, I thought I may have the inattentive subtype of Attention Deficit Hyperactivity Disorder (ADHD), previously known as Attention Deficit Disorder (ADD). Have I gone my whole life undiagnosed? (This is normal actually; many adults get diagnosed with the inattentive subtype in adulthood.) I don't have inattentive subtype (which is ok if you do), I just have too much on my mind. I'm unorganized and easily distracted, because I'm constantly torn to do something else. If my children aren't distracting me, it's my husband, or the dog, or the phone that rings, or the text that I pay attention to instead of finishing what I've originally started. My brain won't shut off to focus on what I'm presently doing.

Mommy Brain Moments

Running late because you can't find your keys.
You find them...

In your PURSE

mom the manager

MICHELLE MCVITTIE

Mommy Brain Moments

When you load the dishwasher

and...

FORGET to TURN IT ON!

mom the manager

> ## Mommy Brain Moments
>
> I just poured milk into the frying pan.
>
> **I REALLY need to FOCUS**
>
> — mom the manager

Mommy Brain Moments

You open the microwave
to find your cold coffee,
that will have to be
reheated for the

THIRD TIME!

Mommy Brain Moments

Got some milk for my coffee.
I noticed a mess, and cleaned the fridge.
I wiped down the counter,
took out the garbage,
and watered the plants.

AND NOW

My coffee is cold and the milk is warm.

mom the manager

So how do you clear your head when it's full of to do lists, negative self-talk, questions to be answered, and thinking about what just happened or what will be happening next. It's about focusing on the task at hand. It's about being organized and being aware when you are getting sidetracked. It's being in the moment, instead of three steps ahead. To be able to work on this you need to be fairly calm. You have to find a way to "turn the volume down on your stress", so you are better able to deal with what comes up in a day. You can't be productive when your stress levels are high. When you function at a six out of ten most days, it doesn't take much for your head to pop off.

Here are a few ideas to get you started.

It takes practice but you can do it!

Practice:
- Relaxation
- Mindfulness
- Positive self-talk
- Slow down, learn to take a pause
- Set goals, make a plan, and write it down!
- Be organized
- Set a routine
- Take it one day at a time
- Learn to say no
- Ask for help, delegate

You have to find a way to "turn the volume down on your stress", so you are better able to deal with what comes up in a day.

> True fulfillment comes from experiences that fill you with joy.
>
> *Collect moments, not things.*

Don't Be So Hard on Yourself

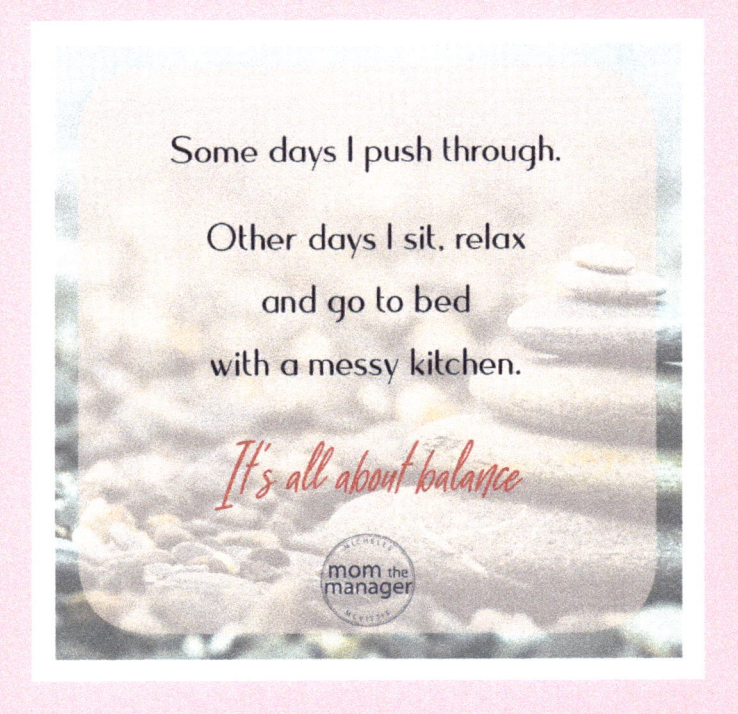

Some days I push through.

Other days I sit, relax and go to bed with a messy kitchen.

It's all about balance

It's none of your business what other people think of you. What matters is how you feel about yourself. If you are surrounded by negativity, then good things will not happen. It starts with you. Tell that annoying jerk inside your head to SHUT THE [INSERT YOUR FAVOURITE SWEAR WORD] UP! Listen to the good things, even if you only believe it fifty percent of the time. The more you do it, the better you'll become.

Think about how far you have come. Are you enjoying the ride? Or are you just going through the motions? Self-esteem isn't something that you can get in a weekend retreat. It's something you work on every day. It's being part of something, feeling like you fit in and being proud of how you contribute to the world. If you aren't feeling that way, you can. It will take time and work, but you will get there. It's going to take some patience and most importantly **self-love**.

Give yourself a break. We all make mistakes, but our mistakes don't define us. Failure is ok; it's what you do with it that matters. Getting back up is what you should focus on. What can you learn from the experience? Put it behind you and move forward. Learn from your mistakes. Depending on what you are moving on from, it may take more time, or help from others. **Figure out what you need and make a plan; take it one step at a time. You got this! You've done it before you can do it again.**

Give yourself a break.
We all make mistakes, but
our mistakes don't define
us. Failure is ok; it's what
you do with it that matters.
Getting back up is what
you should focus on.

> **Be Kind to Yourself**
>
> You are doing your best

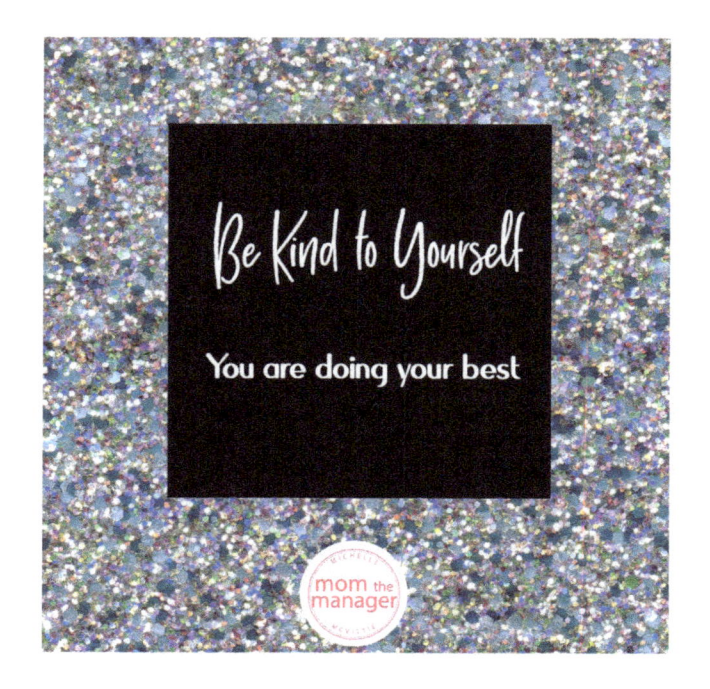

Find Like-Minded People

Find your Joy

Doesn't it feel good to be around people that you can be real with? There is no drama or petty nonsense to deal with. You have the same belief systems, and enjoy the same things. I'm way too old to be dealing with people that don't make me feel good.

It's not too late to meet new people. What are you interested in? Have a business card or mommy card available to hand out so you can connect later. Don't say, "We should get together sometime" and then never follow through. Once you suggest it, then follow up or make a date right then and there.

Host a get-together or a have a play date at your place and invite the other parent to stay. If you are in a relationship or married, how do you re-engage the relationship? So many of us lose touch with why we chose our partner. Life happens and we no longer make our partner or the relationship a priority. Try to fit in time that isn't about the kids, or about chores. Of course those things come up and need to be done, but we need to make time just to hang out and laugh together. What brought you together to begin with? What did you used to do together? Suggest a date, eat meals together, sit and cuddle while watching a show you both like. Relationships are important to have. They lower our stress levels and make us happier people. Alone time is fantastic and necessary. But if you find you are avoiding people, this could be a red flag.

The key word is play!

Play is important for adults as well as children. Do you make time for play? Hang out with friends, go to the water park or amusement park, play a sport, crafting... make sure there's play in your life.

Think Positive

Be grateful for what you have. We tend to focus on the negative. The more negativity we put out into the world the more it is attracted to us. It's hard to make positive changes when we are thinking unhelpful thoughts. **If we think negatively, we feel negative, and we act in unhelpful ways.**

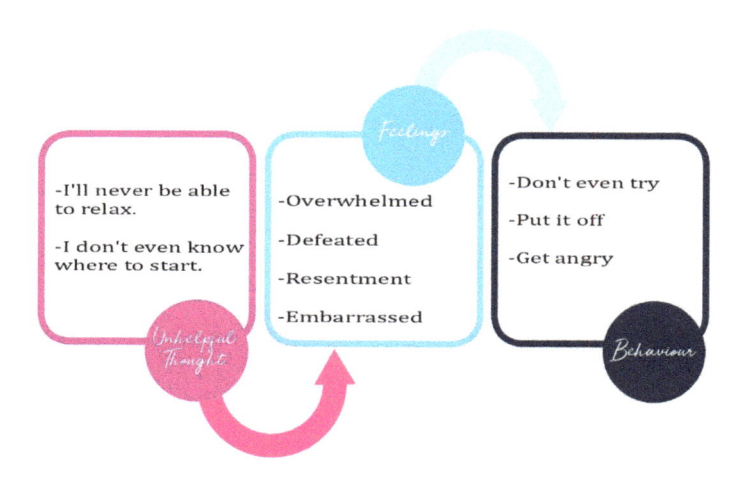

Unhelpful Thought
- I'll never be able to relax.
- I don't even know where to start.

Feelings
- Overwhelmed
- Defeated
- Resentment
- Embarrassed

Behaviour
- Don't even try
- Put it off
- Get angry

You can change the outcome!

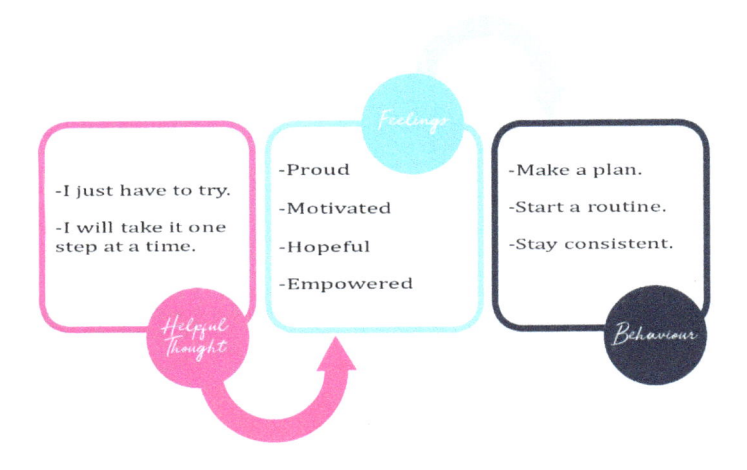

Helpful Thought:
- I just have to try.
- I will take it one step at a time.

Feelings:
- Proud
- Motivated
- Hopeful
- Empowered

Behaviour:
- Make a plan.
- Start a routine.
- Stay consistent.

Our brains automatically turn towards the negative. It's like a muscle – we need to strengthen it to make the positive thought our first instinct. If you start thinking negatively, be aware of it, and change your thinking.

Unhelpful Thought: No one ever listens to me.

Helpful Thought: I can do this today.

Unhelpful Thought: I'm over it!

Helpful Thought: I just need to take a break.

Unhelpful Thought: It's a waste of time.

Helpful Thought: I'll never know if I don't try.

Unhelpful Thought: This will never work.

Helpful Thought: I've done it before, I can do it again.

I'm not saying to be positive and happy all the time – that's unrealistic. I'm rather suspicious of those people who are happy and smiling all the time. I used to work with teenagers who did just that. When you smile all the time, no one asks you questions. If you're happy all the time, people won't see the pain inside.

Eventually it will come out, either by shutting down or exploding. It's finding a balance and learning to get back up when you fall down. Some people find this harder to do than others, but everyone can learn.

Our brains automatically turn towards the negative. It's like a muscle — we need to strengthen it to make the positive thought our first instinct. If you start thinking negatively, be aware of it, and change your thinking.

Find some positive affirmations, thoughts, or motivation from different sources. It could be something your mother used to say to you, something from a song, a movie quote, an affirmation you found online or a saying from a mug or T-shirt. Write it down, put it somewhere you can see it – on your phone, on a sticky note or dry erase board. Put a blank piece of paper in a frame and change the quote each day using a dry erase marker. Be sure to change it often, eventually you won't see it, just like the pile of clothes at the end of the bed.

Here are a few to get you started. Check off the ones you like best:
- Today I choose happiness
- My best is good enough
- I deserve happiness
- I am kind and loving
- Take it one step at a time
- Will this matter in one day, one week or one month?
- Don't always believe what you think
- The time is now
- No one is perfect
- This is going to be a great day
- Everything always works out in the end
- Be patient
- I am a good mother
- I am loved
- I am blessed with…

Famous Quotes for More Inspiration

- "You miss 100% of the shots you don't take."
  —Wayne Gretzky

- "The most difficult thing is the decision to act, the rest is merely tenacity."—Amelia Earhart

- "We become what we think about."
  —Earl Nightingale

- "Life is 10% what happens to me and 90% how I react to it."—Charles Swindoll

- "Winning isn't everything, but wanting to win is."
  —Vince Lombardi

- "I am not a product of my circumstances. I am a product of my decisions."—Stephen Covey

- "Every child is an artist. The problem is how to remain an artist once he grows up."—Pablo Picasso

- "You can never cross the ocean until you have the courage to lose sight of the shore."
  —André Gide (Translation)

- "Either you run the day, or the day runs you."
  —Jim Rohn

- "When one door of happiness closes, another opens; but often we look so long at the closed door that we do not see the one which has been opened for us."
  —Helen Keller

- "No one can make you feel inferior without your consent."—Eleanor Roosevelt

- "Insanity is repeating the same mistakes, but expecting different results."—Narcotics Anonymous

- "A woman is like a tea bag; you never know how strong it is until it's in hot water."
  —Eleanor Roosevelt

There are People Out There Who Can Help You They Make a Living Out of It

Therapy for many is a four-letter word. I've done it, it works. It saved my marriage and my sanity. Therapists don't judge you, they help you look at a situation in a different way. They help you relearn how to react to situations in a healthier way. It's hard work, but it's worth it. There is a huge stigma on not being able to handle things. Just suck it up and move on. Some people are more resilient than others. You may notice it in your family or with your own children. Some people are better able to manage with life's stressors.

The good news is that resilience can be taught. You can learn new ways of thinking and doing things. It takes longer to change habits and behaviours that have been there for years, but it can be done. There is a solution to every problem. Have you always been an anxious person? Do you easily get overwhelmed? Do you hold in your feelings or do you struggle with controlling your temper?

How you cope started in your childhood. I am always talking to parents about self-regulation skills for their children. Many parents realize they lack these skills as well. Wouldn't it have been nice if someone put their arm around you and said it's ok to feel that way, how can we work on this together? Professionals can help you with that today. Start with your family doctor – they need to know about your physical and mental health concerns. They may have a social worker or a therapist as part of their team who can help you.

Therapists are not the only people that can help you, I'm just partial to them because they are my friends, and colleagues, and I know how kind their hearts are. There are many other people you can turn to – it's just finding the right fit. You have to be open and ready to make a change for anything to work.

There is a solution to every problem.

Support groups, hotlines and call centers, websites and online forums, and even apps can be put into action when you have a crisis or just need extra support.

Counselors, spiritual or religious people, holistic practitioners, life coach, expressive arts – vocal, movement, art or music therapy– are a few ideas.

Ask for What You Need

Ask for what you need.

No point waiting for a miracle.

Communication is the key to happiness. The silent treatment is my biggest pet peeve. **If you have something to say, say it!** No one can read your mind. Many disagreements are a result of miscommunication or no communication at all. When you share your thoughts do it respectfully. If talking face to face is too intimidating write it down, send a text. Just please, ASK FOR WHAT YOU NEED! Sorry, I didn't mean to yell, but this is really important.

What do you want the people around you to know? If something upsets you and you keep it to yourself it just sits there. Then something else will pile on top, and then emotions get added to the pile. Then one day, someone looks at you the wrong way, and you freak out. It's never about that "thing" – there is always more to it. When you learn to be assertive and speak up it will save you a lot of difficult feelings.

I am a pleaser – recovering pleaser. I had a hard time sharing how I felt because I didn't like conflict. I didn't want the other person to get upset or get angry with me. Each time I decided to communicate it got easier. I would expect the worst, but it never happened. The other person was always willing to hear what I had to say. It hasn't always been this way. There has been conflict, tears and hurt feelings. How a person responds tells me whether I want to continue a relationship with them. It was hard not to take it personally (sometimes it is personal) but in most cases it is not. I learned to pause before responding, to walk away if they continued talking disrespectfully and/or raising their voice. This is a difficult skill to master, especially keeping your cool and not reacting to the negativity. They could have any emotion they wanted, it didn't mean I needed to own it. It didn't mean I did anything wrong or had to apologize. I used to over apologize, ALL THE TIME. It made everything ok right away, for the other person anyway. It calmed the conflict down and I could feel better. But I didn't feel better; it was a Band-Aid solution.

I learned to tolerate the distress of someone being upset with me. I realized there were some people who just wouldn't hear me out, no matter how valid my response was. I saved myself the time and wasted energy and learned to walk away. I wasn't giving up. I was in charge. I chose myself, not the needs of others. It was liberating.

Don't allow people to treat you poorly, with disrespect. When we engage in the conversation we tell them this is ok. Disengage. Return when you are calm and ONLY if they are worth your time and energy. It can be some hard lessons, but you will see the right path for you. Best to be alone than to be around those that make you feel little and lonely in their presence.

Communication is the key to happiness. If you have something to say, say it! No one can read your mind.

Asking for what you need only works when people are listening

Communication can get muddled with too much talking. We over explain, we let our emotions get in the way and we don't really hear the other person. We want to justify our actions, fix the other person's issue or respond. If you set the example in your home, everyone can start communicating more clearly. Change the way things are done; be the role model your family needs. Asking for what you need only happens if you are being heard. Is your family listening? Do you give them the same respect back? **Listen to understand, NOT to respond.** Sometimes communication is just about listening. A smile or nod can be enough.

Ask for what you need

If you need to be clear about your message or you want your families to be clear with theirs, try these phrases:

"A bug and a wish"

"It bugs me when... I wish you would"

- It **bugs** me when you rush out of the door without saying goodbye. I **wish** you would come and give me a hug before you go.
- It **bugs** me when you want to talk right after an argument. I **wish** you would give me time to calm down.

A bug and a wish works especially well for younger children, but any age could use it.

You can also say: **"This is what I need from you... What do you need from me?"**

- I need you to tell me right away that something is bothering you. What do you need from me?
    - I need you to stay calm and not get upset when I share what is bothering me.
- I need you to help me out with the chores in the home. I'm feeling very overwhelmed and resentful that I'm the only one doing them. What do you need from me?
    - I need to you be ok with how I do it and not fix it or correct the job that I've done.

The key is not to let emotion to take over. Be aware of your emotion. If it gets too intense it's not the right time to be talking. Ask for a break and come back to the conversation when you are calm. You'd be surprised how much things change when you take a break from the situation. Usually, those things that seemed so important and so intense are not as bad as we thought when we were a nine out of ten.

You Don't Have to Do It All

Dear Family,
There is NO kitchen fairy.
It's me.
I'm the kitchen fairy,
and
I QUIT!

mom the manager

I saw a sign the other day that said, "You must be tired watching me clean up after you all day." If they've made a sign you can put on your wall, clearly many people can relate. I've caught myself doing it. I'll be cleaning the kitchen, picking up cups and plates from other rooms, loading the dishwasher. Then my husband puts his cup into the sink and my head pops off! Then I look like the crazy one, the one who overreacts. The problem is, I'd grumble to myself, make comments here and there, but I never actually did anything about my problem. I would come home every day and hope that what I needed to be done would be done. That my husband would see what needed to be done and he would do it. The problem was:

1. I never communicated what I needed.
2. My husband's priorities were usually not the same as mine. (He may have seen cleaning out the garage and getting groceries as the priority, for example. Whereas I would have preferred the laundry and the fridge to be cleaned.)

Help is there – you just have to ask for it. Make a plan, encourage and praise the help you get. When my husband makes me coffee, I text him and say thanks. I don't think, *He better be making me coffee. I make him dinner, wash his clothes and gave him to two beautiful children!* Ok, the thought used to come into my mind. I never used to thank him, why should I? He doesn't thank me for cleaning the floor, folding the laundry or driving the kids to baseball. When I changed my thinking and my behaviour, my life started to change.

Acknowledging and praising good behaviour works for your children and the adults in your life. When my kids are ready for school on time, and we have a great morning, I say, "Way to go, that was a great morning!" I notice when they listen right away, when they do things without being asked, when they behave well and the list goes on. The more you pay attention to good behaviour, the more you'll see it.

Many parents ignore their children when they are quiet, but when they throw something across the room, then they get your attention. You are giving the message that good behaviour gets ignored and bad behaviour gets attention. The same goes for adults. If all I comment on is the bad stuff and ignore the good, no one feels appreciated, and it's all about criticism.

Try not to say, "Thanks for helping me out." Of course they are helping you, but when you put it that way it sounds like they are helping you with "your job".

Help is there, you just have to ask for it. Make a plan, encourage and praise the help you get.

The message should be that we are all working together as a family.

It's just not Mom's house. Have a family meeting and ask them for their ideas on what should be done in the home. When everyone has the opportunity to have their ideas heard there is a better chance for follow through and cooperation.

Delegate!

I'm supposed to be the Manager of my home. So why am I doing **EVERYTHING?**

Sometimes it's easier to do it yourself. If you criticize the way something is done and expect it done a particular way, you are setting yourself up for failure. My grandmother got very upset with me when I criticized my husband's first attempt at cooking chicken. He broiled boneless, skinless chicken breast, with no seasoning. It was dry and tasted like air. I should have been happy he was making the effort, and not focusing on the end result. I took back my negative comments and apologized for the criticism. I gently introduced my husband to a cookbook and encouraged his efforts. I am thankful he tried again. Cooking is now one of his passions, and he's amazing at it. He cooks every holiday meal like it's his job, and I am so grateful for it.

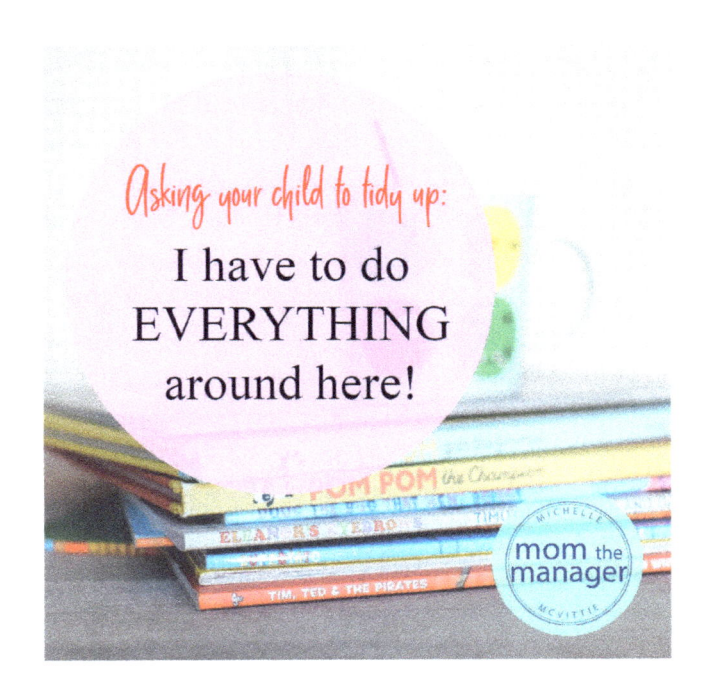

Asking your child to tidy up:
I have to do EVERYTHING around here!

My husband used to have this disease called "I can't fold laundry". FALSE! NO such disease. But I believed he just couldn't do it, so I folded all the laundry. It worked. I would just eventually do it. My children would do it as well. They would complain about helping, I would get irritated with all the whining and I'd just do it for them. **BAD, BAD, BAD idea!** If your children have a reoccurring behaviour, it's because it's working for them!

When you change how you react, your family's behaviours will start to change. Some might resist this change and push back. But, if you remain consistent it will work.

Make a plan. Get a visual, like a chart or check list. Have clear expectations and follow through. My children get ready for school on their own. They make their own breakfast and lunch and walk to school. A whole kilometre there and back, and they are alive to talk about it. My son told me I got in the way in the morning, so I backed off. I took more time upstairs on my own. Mornings are amazing! No more screaming! My children feel empowered. They are learning valuable life skills and independence. We work together so we have more time for family time. I feel less frustration and resentment, because everyone is pitching in. I acknowledge all contributions, no matter how small, it's all paying off. I'm a very proud mom.

Make a plan. Get a visual, like a chart or check list. Have clear expectations and follow through.

Anything is Possible
You Just Have to Try

Take the First Step

mom the manager

It starts today! Find your balance. Find your passion. Find your true self. Motherhood is only part of who you are. It is a wonderful part, the best in fact. But there are so many other characteristics about yourself you can discover and develop. Use positive words when talking about your goals and aspirations. Remove words such as **No** and **Can't.** Remind yourself each day that you deserve to be happy. You deserve to have a healthy balance in your life.

I've given you a lot of suggestions to try; it's up to you to choose what strategies will work the best for you. No matter what you decide, be patient with yourself and the process. Take it one day at a time.